COLUMBIA COLLEGE CHICAGO

3 2711 00162 2079

W9-CNF-978

THE LIONS

AUG 1 8 2009

PHOENIX POETS

COLUMBIA COLLEGE LIBRARY
600 S. MICHIGAN AVENUE
CHICAGO, IL 60605

The Lions

PETER CAMPION

THE UNIVERSITY OF CHICAGO PRESS *Chicago and London*

PETER CAMPION is assistant professor of English at Auburn University and editor of *Literary Imagination.* His first book of poems, *Other People,* was published in the Phoenix Poets series by the University of Chicago Press in 2005.

The University of Chicago Press, Chicago 60637
The University of Chicago Press, Ltd., London
© 2009 by The University of Chicago
All rights reserved. Published 2009
Printed in the United States of America

18 17 16 15 14 13 12 11 10 09   1 2 3 4 5

ISBN-13: 978-0-226-09310-9 (paper)
ISBN-10: 0-226-09310-7 (paper)

Library of Congress Cataloging-in-Publication Data
Campion, Peter, 1976–
    The lions / Peter Campion.
        p. cm. — (Phoenix poets)
    ISBN-13: 978-0-226-09310-9 (cloth : alk. paper)
    ISBN-10: 0-226-09310-7 (cloth : alk. paper)
    I. Title.
    PS3603.A486L5 2009
    811'.6—dc22

                                2008025561

♾ The paper used in this publication meets the minimum requirements of the American National Standard for Information Sciences—Permanence of Paper for Printed Library Materials, ANSI Z39.48-1992.

for Amy and Jack

Contents

THREE

Acknowledgments

I want to thank the editors of the following journals in which these poems first appeared:

Agenda (U.K.) : "Invisible Bird," "The Great Divide" (in an earlier version)
Agni: "Recurring Dream in a New Home"
Art New England: "Bad Reception," "Invisible Bird"
Blackbird: "The Lions"
The New Hampshire Review: "Protest"
The New Republic: "Simile"
Poetry: "Big Avalanche Ravine," "In Late August," "Just Now," "Magnolias"
Poetry Northwest: "In Early March," "September," "So Here Is How We Live Now"
Slate: "Lilacs"

"Big Avalanche Ravine" and "Magnolias" appeared in *Contemporary Poetry 4* (South Korea) with translations into Korean and an accompanying essay by Joon-Soo Bong.

An earlier version of "The Presidio: After Morning Thunder" was issued as a letter press broadside, printed at Greenwood Press, in affiliation with the Bonnafont Gallery, San Francisco, CA.

For their comments on earlier versions of this book, I owe particular gratitude to Amy Campion, David Ferry, Jed Perl, Deborah Rosenthal, Tom Sleigh, Joshua Weiner, and C. K. Williams.

ONE

In Early March

It happens in our ignorance.
Fringing the steep calderas and
sinkholes
          the blacktail deer descend.
Trembling. All systems on alert.
White concrete banks of the reservoirs
then corridors of power lines
fall to this circuitry
                  this chain
like the channels through silicon.
Though our estrangement from
nature means nothing to them.
And past our mist of sentiment
they also are barest presences.

Ancient and ahistorical with sunlit
mucous dribbling off their snouts

they hold us in their vitreous
unblinking eyes however long.

Then tense. Then pulse out through the air
smelling of buckwheat and water.

Embarcadero

Enormous woman
in her orange blazer

bike messenger
dangling his wire

spare change or
lilies in cellophane:

the entire current holds
its edges even while spilling

into the future
And the exhaust it trails

(newspaper
leer of the President)

seems to fuse with want
with this granular

sunlight on curved skin
gossamer hair

outlandish
turquoise on leopard print

    *   *   *

Bliss and anger fear and
wonder   they revolve so fast

there must be
somewhere beyond them

some landscape whose
contours arrive and sharpen

in lucent particular
Only to picture it

pulls up these
streets at evening:

smell of bread or
drizzle on pavement

and billboards for bacon and
cell phones glisten:

beautiful people
bound by the bright clothes

the animal of them
seems about to break from

Bad Reception

It was the average newscast footage.
Out the breech of an M-16, shell casings cut
a golden arc across the picture.

In the background, palm fronds. Maybe some stucco.
The embedded mouth, speaking American.
Then the pixels went fuzzy and

one more image wired up to our kitchen
disappeared. Though the outlines lingered, swelled.
In the office or crossing a jet bridge or

turning from the road to catch the pink
explosions of ice plant. . . . It keeps on circling
back to me: that ragged ballistic spray.

It feels like charging up, getting high:
the images whack through deserts and towns
while the men take fire, and the sheer

velocity of the emotion, thumping
through the bloodstream, feels unstoppable.
Then it grows cold and clear, all that anger

a polluted overspill. The drying basil
and the radio and the evening showers
leaving the eucalyptus liquid with sun.

My entire life in this household with her.
How infinitesimal we are, hidden here
inside the sweep of what we will not stop.

Magnolias

Ambition. Jealousy. Adrenaline.
The fear that loneliness is punishment
and that corrosive feeling draining down
the chest the natural and just result
of failures. . . . What delicious leisure not
to feel it. What sweet reprieve to linger
here with these ovals of purple and flamingo
plumed from the tree or splayed on pavement.
If only for these seconds before returning
to the open air those flowers keep
pushing out of themselves to die inside.

Capitalism

after Jin Eun Young

Darkened arcade
strobed with colors   or

a million kilometer tunnel

centipeding

over the ocean floor:

how will I walk through here alone?

Scrapbook: 2006

1. *July*

Another summer in America.
And again this sense that everything is large
and clear
        but also smothered: honeyed over
with a too languorous forgetfulness.

Spritzing the trellised morning glories. Reading.
Driving the strip. . . . We're fully here, engaged.
Except the hours bleed to heat mirage.

Along the bar last night, the usual clank
and chatter, for a second, pinged and echoed.
Up on the screens an amateur video panned

whatever word they used for torture chamber.

Under the anchor's voice (what I most remember)
seeming the deepest presence in the world:

the original, rhythmic wheeze of the cameraman.

11. *From Above the Great Divide*

Like the tables and dressers Parkman found
past Council Bluffs in grass along the Platte:
fine English craftsmanship left blistering.

Or like resorts off season: puffed cloudscape
sweeping above the puddled swimming pools.

Sometimes the wastefulness seems beautiful:

as if sheer want could make a person clean.
It lingers underneath the tedium
of airplane travel, that unquenchable

glitter of freedom: shining from the snow
and rock below it says you are allowed

to leave the crinkling web of bonds behind
and step entirely outside your life

because no loss is unsustainable.

III. *Best and the Brightest*

The dream was like a funnel: swivelling
through purple, closer and closer to the center.
Fires down the barricaded boulevards.
Machine guns in the airport terminals.

Then I was seated at a tracklit table.
Our committee's tie pins and cufflinks chimed.
Dan Johnson, my whiz kid classmate, was with me.

It felt collegiate. Our debate cantered on
in rational tones, while past the sentences
the terror snaked and flared through night untouched.

At last it was Dan's turn.
                              And all that came
was garble: "In the Reagan era. . . . No. . . .
The ballistics plan. . . ." Smiles flashed polite dismissal.

Then the click and spin of their briefcase latches.

iv. *At The Seoul Writers' Festival*

Riot police hustle in shield formation
past the American Embassy while we chat.
From the tour bus it seems pure spectacle.
We pass round soju in a thermos cap.

One row back the Korean student aide
prods the Filipino about his girlfriend:
"How does she look like?"
                                        She cajoles him
for a photo.
                    Though on leaflets tomorrow
we'll see the nightsticked demonstrators dripping

blood on the pavement. And another aide
will tell me, gently: "It's not you we hate."

Right now, only the tubular glow of the bus.
Digital blips on the window. And English:

"How does she look like?
                    O . . . beautiful."

v. *Imperium*

Our largeness. Like an overbearing child's
or parent's. Pixilated brand names and
pop stars pleading across the firmament.

Which says nothing of fire power.

It feels like doing eighty on the freeway
as little towns agglomerate and blur:

all smallness turns unreal. The neighborhoods
are merely stations everyone is leaving.

And under the dark trees at the reservoirs

lovers still give themselves away all summer.

As if some feared departure quickened them
they search each other's faces . . . :

                              such small creatures

under the condo gleam and the bleared stars.

The Great Divide

From his desk your father asked for you
that Christmas morning. He explained. Last night

your mother " . . . passed." You would be leaving now
for boarding school. The silence of that ride

across Ohio echoed down our family.
You were eleven. And you must have been

already swathing with your Christian patience
the impassive severity that sunk

the foundations of that house and echoed
in your firm "on Earth as it is in Heaven."

Now you are the deserted reservoir
children bushwhack across to glimpse

beyond their terraced roofs. The long sweep
to the Great Divide. The moonscape of Utah.

The solitude of running lights descending
High Sierra curves through the snowpack.

Like the Indian names denial absorbs
into the landscape severed from blood:

you died into me and many others. And
we carry you in silence not even thinking.

At crosswalks sliced by the long horizon.
In the swarm of the concourse. You burn

in that loneliness. In the passing faces.
Their cycles of departure and fierce arrival.

So Here Is How We Live Now

with so much power propelled beyond us
that it seems almost unreal to be together
scissoring past the fountain on Market Street.

Your words are agile bursts inside the marble
flash and billow. Your kiss an exact spot
of wet heat melting along my cheek.

But beneath the moment a streak of nerve end
shudders: saying that nothing lasts except
the current ripping us away from here.

                    *   *   *

One image keeps edging the distracted

scatter: that river we watched last fall.
Off Highway 49
                    at Convict Flat
descending to the canyon past staggered walls

of metamorphic slate and the steep shale
it collected in long pools. And collected
all its surroundings: nests of abandoned wire

and elephant ear and alders ranked beside
the riffles where starlings pecked their akimbo wings.
Then beneath the seams and eddies, first as

thin blue ellipses, it hurdled forward.
Frothed arabesques. White roar of the tail race.
Smashing off laddered boulders, all that force

falling through air.

* * *

             That feeling of a substance
emptied . . . it runs the deepest when dark comes on.
The offices are floating yellow cubes.

Prices at closing sluice their windows.
You are a slender reflection on plate glass.

And then sheer presence: dream and warmth and speech.

Driving now: the bridge's funneled lunge
and shudder toward Oakland.
                  Eyes on the road
we're walled to ourselves.
                And still it pours

around us: this invisible course we carve

although our lives have separate ends. This blind
plunge where again and again we find each other.

The Presidio: After Morning Thunder

The eucalyptus pomped to a tropical
huge wall. But fraying to ragged swoops
   along the tops, beneath a thinned out
      cumulus rumple. What a strange calm.
This sense of being no one and nowhere.
Yet here is this sunburned mom.
                       Her jumpsuit.
  Her English Terrier snuffling the runneled
    mulch.
         The world is bare material.
Accrual. Ballooning outlines the sun
descends along
             implying the surface life
of dental work and payment plans and
   summer vacations with Pop at Tahoe.

Brash morning we all have arisen to:
" . . . Now Joe with our Metro Traffic Report! . . ."

And then the storm wind's fluent rumor.

It tastes of ocean.
           Stretches of molten sun
out past the Farallons. Undulant purplish tones.

It thins then circles back. It carries
   always that almost unconscious hint

that there must be
              somewhere beyond us:
some nowhere space where we are volumes and voids:

  resplendent pulp and viscous shadow
    spiraled from air and yet to take on names.

Invisible Bird

This moment, in this waking drift, a wren
keeps calling from some imperceptible

hideout on the spruce beside our window.
Two notes. The first's a clarion slice through air.

The second's lower though. The frequency
carries more body in it. Ringing down

through flesh and bone itself the second note
seems to release some baleful knowledge: echoing

that trill with so much resonance, it circles
back to its source the way the self returns

to make a home of the space around it.
What a cowl of illusion. What a morose

raiment of tattered reassurances
to slouch inside. But it works.

The cover lifts. The world comes clear again.
And the body will stand out shivering

if need be. Claw through garbage if need be.

Simile

The way on green alluvial islands where the Zambezi meets the Cuando

the lions (cubs scanning smudged horizons as the father drops his snout in gore)
shake out a clump of vertebra and sinews in their teeth to extract the sweetest meat

so we might call it "merciless":
                                like that we rip reality from all the surfaces that flow

around us. And live in the amnesia of our doing it (I do) and so no end.

TWO

In Late August

In a culvert by the airport
under crumbling slag
wine colored water seeps
to this pool the two does
drink from: each sipping as
the other keeps look out.
The skyline is a wash
of barcode and microchip.
Even at home we hold
the narrowest purchase.
No arcs of tracer fire.
No caravans of fleeing
families. Only this
suspicion ripples
through our circles of lamp glow
(as you sweep the faint sweat
from your forehead and flip
another page in your novel)
this sense that all we own
is the invisible
web of our words and touches
silence and fabulation
all make believe and real
as the two does out
scavenging through rose hips
and shattered dry wall:

their presence in the space
around them liveliest
just before they vanish.

1980: Iran

At first the demonstration seemed
far off: a caterpillar
brushing against the buildings.

Then the cameras were inside.
The bodies clustered and our flag
danced upward in transparent flames

the kerchiefed faces scattered from
but also keep approaching, tranced.
I remember how this

constrictive chill
wrapped down my ribs
each time they played the clip.

It snaked against an emptiness
the way the bodies spiked
around their rags of flapping ash.

The shock of signals said to bite
or burrow to protect that
central core. And then was gone.

The coldness must have seeped beneath
the plush of assurance.
                              Purple
leaves of the maple brushing

our window.
                    "Strawberry Fields"
on the Hi Fi. John Lennon's
"Let me take you down. . . ."

as the tricycle

zoomed me through amber halls.
The world had amplitude.

Then the sound
of my parents in another room.
Their battling a whip lash

of operatic gush and silence.

In snatches as the fabric ripped
it seemed so clear: the dread that clawed me

watching the fire eat the colors

out of the demonstrators' hands
. . . it said that home was sacred:

beyond opinion or belief
the center of the self (that made
all foreign powers enemies.)

And if the fighting meant

abasement   cruelty   disguise

I would need to fight for it.

Just Now

a lady bug, its carapace blown open
so a translucent trace of orange gleams
from its body, has ascended link by link
the smudgy silver curve of my watchband.
It must have helicoptered past the sill
while I was slumped here squinting in the paper
at the ashen packaging another bombing's
made of a minivan. Made available
in the photo like the homeless in a poem.
The pain is far away. But then for moments
utterly clear: molten metal guttering
down from the Milky Way to fall on us.
And sometimes, God, it lands with all its will.
My spluttered prayer for it to hold its distance:
how ludicrous to blurt if from this comfort.
Still it impels itself from me. Please stay
away from me. Please stay away from this
insectile soul who only weeks ago
was wind and shit and jasmine leaves and rain.

1989: Death on the Nile

Shot from a helicopter over Cairo
our hotel pool would be a turquoise drop.

I've learned to see like that, imagining
each place we travel through from somewhere else.

Right now, my mother and her journalist
boyfriend glisten beneath their sunscreen.

Their life together is a giddiness
they surface from (like coming through the door

between hotel rooms) to attend to me
and my brother. Here with us they need to click

the edges of the puzzle back in place.
Yes it's a privilege to travel. Yes

we're guests of the Egyptian government.
Portraits of Hosni Mubarek follow us.

But earlier, as the cool Mercedes inched
into the souq (the smell of cigarettes

then sewage and saffron) why did I register
the river of faces only as phantoms?

Even my body seemed to freeze away
the present, as my shallow breathing trickled

its supplies to its distant client states.
Right now, the pool sends sunlight crumpling

across the pages of my mystery.
But in the sentences, Hercule Poirot

in his labyrinth of death and art deco
seems more real. Even slapping the book down

and loafing back through the Little Europe
of our hotel (past marble columns, djellabas

and sharp Chanel) I can almost replace
the present. Fantasia of passageways.

A gun barrel peeking from palm fronds.
Blood leaking down the palatial staircase.

And then the make believe dissolves.
The elevator's polished gold distorts

my face to glops of biomorphic syrup.
So many years before the words arrive.

Before I pull it back as memory.
I want to scream. To claw the surfaces.

Quavering through the doorway, I collapse
on the bed to wish my rage away as nausea

washes in waves through the open blue.
Invisible to me, the Nile

gathers all surfaces in its reflections.
The ancient neon Coca Cola sign.

Goats bleating from the mud-brick roofs. A whiff
of spearmint tea and kef. My mother dipping

toes then calves in the turquoise. The agent
sent here from Langley haunting his beach umbrella.

Info he zapped from beneath the electrodes.
Right now, right now, right now . . . as the dry heaves

leave me wet and cool on the bathroom tiles:
how inescapable the present feels.

Right now, right now, right now. . . . Not like a novel
hiding me in its chambered structure. No:

the day is here. It is the single thing
I need to make my life inside: its forward

spiral, constant and rapid as the river
charging from Aswan to Alexandria.

Lethe

Three times he tried to throw his arms around
his father's neck. Three times his father slipped
his grasp: weightless as air or shapes in dreams.
And then he saw a valley fall away.
Secluded groves. The waving leaves and shoots.
And cleaving that peacefulness: the River Lethe.
People from every race, innumerable, swarmed
in circles there: the way the bees in summer
hover past clumps of flowers but home in
on the lilies, dribbling off their white fur
and making meadow after meadow murmur.

Tensed and chilled from his vision, in ignorance
the hero asked what river was that there?
Who were those people crowding the slick bank?

His father answered:
                    "Souls who have more lives
to enter numb their pain with this water.
This is the river of oblivion.

So many times I've wanted you to come and
see the linked chain of our children's children.
Which will deepen both our contentment
when you reach your final destination."

"How is this true? The souls here rise through heaven
only to plummet into bodies once again?
What makes them so ravenous for daylight?"

His father said, "My son, I'll show you."
And he unfolded each detail in order.

"First the heavens and earth, then lakes and oceans
then the resplendent globes of the moon and sun
and stars are infused with spirit: all bound

by the same intelligence that blends them.
From spirit flow all men and animals.
And birds. And even those monsters with scales

and fins beneath the marbled ocean surface.
Fire is the force that falls from upper air
and charges them with life: however much

brute random matter doesn't leech from them
or else their earthbound frames detract from them.
And so they fear and crave. Rejoice and mourn.

They can't discern the prisons they live in.
Even when life sputters away from them
so many cripplings ingrained in them

remain. They're driven into punishment
to cleanse themselves. Some hang full length
above a windblown emptiness. Some purge

infection under floods, or scouring fire.
We suffer in the ways our lives have led us.
And then we're sent through wide Elysium

where just the slimmest number make their homes.
The others, when they've spun the wheel of time
a thousand years, are summoned in their swarms

to these wet banks. And here they slake their thirst.
Bleaching their memories, they glimpse the sky
once more. And hunger for bodies to move inside."

New Hampshire:
Lake at the Back of Memory

Mist on the darker water
over the circle of buoy rope

erratic slap of
smallmouth snatching

moths from the surface film

The real lake
may fleck some

gated ring of condos now
and even so

it shimmers there
this hole in time   this

spring your life has
spilled from for years

not even knowing
but in moments

sliced from dream

* * *

Exultant
or suffering

it drizzles down the same:

calves
flashing above black water

silted emerald
off fingertips

and as if
            emulsified
eternities

with rock and milk and

stars
        the entrance
into the world again

white lifeguard chair

half moon
and the sodium glow

crackles off dripping skin

Big Avalanche Ravine

Just the warning light on a blue crane.
Just mountains. Just the mist that skimmed
them both and bled to silver rain
lashing the condominiums.
But there it sank on me. This urge
to carve a life from the long expanse.
To hold some ground against the surge
of sheer material. It was a tense
and persistent and metallic shiver.
And it stayed, that tremor, small and stark
as the noise of the hidden river
fluming its edge against the dark.

Lilacs

It used to burn, especially in spring:
the sense that life was happening elsewhere.

Smudged afternoons when lilacs leaked their smell
past schoolyard brick, whole plotlines seemed to twist

just out of reach. Inside the facing houses
chamber on networked chamber rose . . . to what?

Some angel chorus flowing around the sun?
Some lurid fuck? . . . For years that huge desire

simmered, then somehow . . . didn't dissipate
so much as fuse itself to thought and touch.

This May, our life is here, a branching center.
Freeways and cellular towers and the blue

avenues at dusk with their scuttle and blur.
They all, if just for seconds, fall away.

You stand in purple shade beside your dresser.
And filtering off the park the breeze returns it:

lilac: its astringent sweetness, circling us
as if it were fulfillment of desire.

But not fulfillment. Just the distance here
between us, petaled, stippling to the touch.

THREE

Sparrow

With its swift
flick and plummet
through the chrism
of these first hours
after the rain
spraying droplets
off its wingtips then
scissoring past
the phone lines
into the blue
distance of roofs
and freeways
how not see it as
diving past
all we slather
onto the world
diving past it
the same way
we survive
our happiness
and also: sorrow.

Protest

They showed us on the evening news. Our breath
was visible. So our chants appeared as impish
volleys of vapor as the camera panned.

But for those moments we were beautiful creatures.
Have you ever seen, in person, horses lined up and stamping?
Ranked by the glowing snowbanks, our bodies

buckled against the gates. We were a timed
explosion of sinew and snap, the jagged force
of our convictions: even if we knew

screaming for peace was mere charade, the words
made palpable this threshold: this pop
of some lever catching, of some catch releasing.

* * *

There are the suppressed reports. There is
a captain telling of villagers he befriended.
How he returned to find them kneeling in a line.

How a sergeant from another unit opened fire.
How his superior held the captain back
with his clipped, bureaucratic "no can do"

as the shots and pleading ripped the air.
Those pages must lie in an archive. Those fibrous
spaces between the type. Their meager glow.

* * *

Only an hour ago when I caught the outlined
family faces in frames by the window
. . . . How to explain? How wrench to words?

Outside, the lights of gantries and cranes by the water.
The netted system we all were tangled in.
My brother's face there, and my father's mother's

portrait from years ago. So tenuous
the links. My skin was wholly taken over
by my pulse, and my pulse was streaming so fast

I wondered, if it were cut, what scrubbing would it
take to clean the blood from the floor boards.

Recurring Dream in a New Home

Sumac and shadow of the girder bridges.
Then the downtown where a fountain's iron swan

gurgles white gouts. Beyond the buggy edges
fraying the green, the darkness switches on.

Solid as cups of buttermilk they stand
beside their Pontiac. Her polka dots

rumple and shine in the moonlight. His hand
pats a pocket for something he forgot.

I fumble toward them: "Nana! Boppa! It's me!
.... We have our own son now!" They turn and stare

as if they sense someone they can't quite see.
And then they've given up. They're in their car.

Taillights smudge mist. And all they've left behind
is their image: the pudgy rectitude

of retirees venturing half blind
into their lives, not knowing what's ahead

except the increasing toil of taking on
bodies again, each morning, as the dark

slinks off behind the buildings and the sun
drips from the cars and trash and steaming bark.

The Lions

At first it's just a mist: a neural drizzle
priming the sense of summer dusk and ocean.
Then memory filters down the colors.
Nana stands swathed in electric green.
She has me carrying coats to the shuttered
shade of the living room. The patio hums.
Glasses chime through the flash and clatter.

As if wavering between relief
and disappointment, she cinches her lips.
One line remains unchecked on her guest list.
She mumbles to the air: ". . . Well, they'll be missed."
The perfumed coats lie sleeve to sleeve, complete.

So I was free.
       The lucent harbor side
those nights (and this one lingers most)
became a reef: a sprawl of hidden life.

I hungered for a narrative. . . . The blur
of bodies shadowed on the screened-in porches.
Their conversation clumped to one murmur
from behind the sputtering garden torches.
They had that allure of murder mysteries.
I pictured sneaking in there. Prowling through
the moonlit hallways, knowing what to seize.
Somewhere the clues lay hidden in plain view.

I imagined a lion in Botswana
coiled in his lunge, suspended there, then landing
on a scuttle of freaked gazelles. His claws
were regulators, rulers of the flow.
Reality lay hot beneath him, steamed
from the spill of entrails smutting his nose.
Then the flow had fled and the world had changed.
Less than the meadows change beneath the clouds
but still: this sense of impending emptiness.

I must have seen it on a nature show.
The harborside itself was like a screen
I played those looped scenarios across:
those doors into the dark like fired glass
molten and coursing. Then transparent again.
And there was only me. Our driveway shone
beneath the pines. Inside my metal pail
the fish called scup, their dorsal fins a clump
of spikes, flashed silver at the alien air.

II.

Again tonight I play the DVD.

In Technicolor blue the sonar men
watch contacts pulse across their screen.
The soundtrack is ambient flutes and rain.

War without end is about to begin
again. The green of the far off shoreline
quivers and glints.
                    Then McNamara's voice
(its chopping, crowlike nasal): "I was part
of a mechanism. . . . I was part. . . ."
                                        Again I feel
this expectant thrill. As the flute notes swerve
and his wooden pointer slaps his map
of the Bay of Tonkin
                        I see our harborside.
The dripping honeysuckle and rosehips.

It seems ethereal. As if the leaves
brushing the houses against the dark shore
were opening. The space they make cleaves
the shadowed walls. Becomes a trembling core.

A piercing stinging. Dim retinal trace
of languorous curves, uncovered hips and breasts.

And then it's gone. I'm slouching on our couch
watching two F-4 Phantoms swoop then strafe.

Only the sting remains.
                              "Vietnam":
the very sound the slice then hum of pain.

How obvious it seems: those nights marauding
yard to yard through the ivy beds . . . the secret
fenced from view was the failure of their war.
Swirling around the grown-ups with their drinks
the threat of its acknowledgment
                                        was the gulp
of that impending emptiness: as close
as the white noise of trees above the harbor.

Caught in the minima of new reports
"on CLL in veterans exposed
to the herbicide known as Agent Orange":

my uncle
              ghosting the house that summer bald
from chemo.
                  Or the boy my aunt adored
in high school.
                      How his name once fell
in conversation. Sudden uneasiness.
Branch shadows serrating the patio.

Then one of them caught the drop with
rueful amusement, telling how he clomped
straight through the glass wall of the Bauhaus
arts center.
                  How my father and his friends
stood round in wonder as he shed
the pane, its shattered, clattering cascade.

III.

Claws clicking down the maple halls, the lions
circled our house. Svelte messengers of dream
they leapt the countertops or lounged against
the fireplace with swish indifference.
Whatever terror lay behind them wasn't there.
But glistened still. Those nights meandering
sleep's borderlands
                    and now, calling them back:
they flaunt their elegance, their cool comportment
of cocktail hour royalty
                    (all surfaces
maintained)
                    which makes the flare of violence
cut to the bone more quickly:
                              blood-smeared tongues
lapping their mangled kill on Nana's rugs.

IV.

The one line unchecked on the guest list.
This family lore I delve through all the more
for its eeriness.
                    My mother's parents met
in 1938 on Beacon Hill.
They were towelling off champagne flutes and humming
show tunes at Robert McNamara's sink.

The thrill (all three had grown up poor)
must have cut the rush of approaching war.

And the decades falling
                        like my parents falling
out of love.
            In the shadow of the leaves
blending to black above the patio

their present starts to read as a prelude.
Or afterwards.
                And Nana's Julia Childish
promptings (her piercing alto "ah"s) go shrill:

desperate loopings and cinchings to hold fast
our story line inside the growing darkness.

Her invitation zipped across the Sound
to the World Bank President's summer home
was a sheer lark.
                    We were anonymous.

And the decades falling
                    like the numbers
plummeting now across my TV screen and
zapping each city's casualties to stats.

They hide the girl in the famous shot who runs
right down the center of the highway naked
dangling her arms as if to shake off
some especially terrible nightmare
though what she's shaking are flags of flesh.

Shots on a screen.
                    But how immediate
that voice, biting through now:
                                        ". . . I was
part of a mechanism . . . I was part . . ."
The obvious logic of history
grinds down inside of it: no him, no me.

And my anger against the propped up surfaces:

my rage to rip through to the other side

and the fear that all that waited there
was emptiness:
                    even now as tracers flare
to pixels
            those unstanchable currents ride
my sprawl of nerves
                    while Jack and Amy sleep
and passing headlights swivel round our ceiling.

v.

Dim underbrush. The lions smudged
to brownish yellow clumps in the foliage.
A couple, circling, grow clearer now.
Their liquid pink yawns. White flash of fang.
Dissolving like a dream, the picture bleeds.
Uphill from the harbor, I'm standing on mildewed
planks to the beach house.

                      Could it really have been
that same night?

              I drop the pail of fish
and slouch to the entrance. The salt air makes
fresh water puddled by the showers smell fresher.

No lions nuzzling each other's manes and necks.
But stretching on a spread of towels: a woman.

I can see her strawberry pubic hair
beneath her t-shirt.

                And a man is coming
out from the shadows kneeling over her.
It happens so fast, their blur of rupture:
like that, he's thrusting into her. Her thighs
have butterflied around his waist: they squeeze
then slacken.

              Their faces simmer in the plaques of
late sun through the window.

                      I don't know them.
Only I see: that this is violence.
Only a kind they don't deny but relish:
diving inside of it again, teeth clenched.

And their striving.
               And the tensed but molten feeling
circling my chest.
               A force behind all motion.

Coiled in then bursting forward, it unfolds
itself through time. Then this, then this, then this:
life happening, each instant, rivers history.
Or nothing. Blankness between small lucid splotches.

At the church in D.C. my infant mother
cradled in Robert McNamara's arms.
His spectacles two pendant discs of light.
His parted, slicked back hair. The priest intones
the liturgy for Catholic godparents:
"The saving water is your tomb and womb . . ."

Then this, then this, then this. East Asia plumed
with chemical fire. Me sitting here.
The images half unreal through the televised wash.
But the smaller pain the larger links to:
next to me, on the plastic monitor
the syncopated phosphorescent beads
tracking Jack's sleeping breathing now
open their little waterfall of nerves:
this need to clutch our bond of family

while the funneling drub of force
crashes and spumes.
                              Out there in the world
people ride elevators with glassed views
of warehouse blocks and freeways unfurling
into the treetops.
                       People walk the blue
checkpointed tunnels to missile silos.
                                   And to pull
against it, tearing through the surface, feels
impossible.
                  Unless some animal
intelligence, sharp toothed, could slice a path.

I mean the force I saw that night, before
I broke and ran.
                       It's clear in memory.
She's striding him now. Her eyes are closed.

She pushes down, then stretches up, as if
she's pulling out of her that power

gathering in her enraged yet delicate
cascade of shattered "oh"s:
                              that creature
released to make its home now as the night falls
among the broken sheets of sizzling surf
and the honeysuckle dripping and rosehips.

Display Copy

after Nan Goldin

Down on their towels, stoned, the couple stares
toward light of the year and month I was born.
Horny, or existentially forlorn:
tough to tell. Their faces soak the glare
off dunes behind them, so whatever look
they're wearing bleaches out.
                                    But neither blinks.
And four blue eyes when the shutter clicks
show clear as water pooling in a brook
while land and sky blot white.
                                    The shading gives
the feeling that they're utterly withdrawn
from where they are. But the town name's printed on
the bottom: part of my family still lives
and two are buried there.
                                    It must be
one of those beaches my mother took me to:
leading up splintered walks until the view
opened below.
                    Wide span of lavender sea.
And always those casual emergencies
of families, kids scrambling round the chairs
with their pails. And always someone's covert stares
(like this couple's) from the bleached peripheries.

Most of these photo art books on display
hide public secrets. Men in chaps who tie
each other down. One woman's blood-rimmed eye.
The stitchwork on the bindings starts to fray
from all the handling.
                              Glancing round the store
then back, I skimmed until I found this shot.
It's not like transport in some cloudbanked thought.
It's just the fact of them and nothing more.
The fact is like a shock.
                              They're in that time and place
and staring out at me. The sweeping sand
is so immaculate that their figures stand
out strangely. They are the shapes that they erase.

No way of knowing if they're still alive.
Or where they live. Or who they have become.

The aisles are crowded now. Voices thrum
from the stairwell. People leave, arrive
and leave again.
                              Their passing faces glint
in high res from the rush of surfaces
then flow back into it. That's how it is:

they flow back into it, and then they don't.

September

How clean
the thousand surfaces
rivers
      RVs and
orange mesas
             emerge each morning
rows of privet
clipped and swept

a linen blouse uncreased beneath
the steaming iron

again and again
the world is rinsed
to a scintillant mesh

And still
      the faces
gush from arrival gates
throbbing with this
bare imperative

to populate
the shivering expanse
this drive